ONE DAY MORE

A PLAY IN ONE ACT

JOSEPH CONRAD

TRUE SIGN
PUBLISHING HOUSE

Published by True Sign Publishing House
Address: SY. No. 21/2 & 21/3, Sonnenahalli,
Krishnarajapura, Bengaluru,
Karnataka - 560049 India
E-mail: truesignbooks@gmail.com
Website: www.truesign.in

One Day More A Play In One Act
Author: Joseph Conrad

ISBN: 978-93-5584-348-7

First Edition: 2023

CONTENTS

CHARACTERS

Captain Hagberd (a retired coasting skipper).

Josiah Carvil (formerly a shipbuilder—a widower—blind).

Harry Hagberd (son of Captain Hagberd, who as a boy ran away from home).

A Lamplighter.

Bessie Carvil (daughter of Josiah Carvil).

SCENE

A small sea port

To right, two yellow brick cottages belonging to Captain Hagberd, one inhabited by himself the other by the Carvils. A lamp-post in front. The red roofs of the town in the background. A sea-wall to left.

Time: The present-early autumn, towards dusk.

ONE DAY MORE

SCENE - I

CURTAIN RISES DISCLOSING CARVIL and Bessie moving away from sea-wall. Bessie about twenty-five. Black dress; black straw hat. A lot of mahogany-coloured hair loosely done up. Pale face. Full figure. Very quiet. Carvil, blind, unwieldy. Reddish whiskers; slow, deep voice produced without effort. Immovable, big face.

Carvil (Hanging heavily on Bessie's arm). Careful! Go slow! (Stops; Bessie waits patiently.) Want your poor blind father to break his neck? (Shuffles on.) In a hurry to get home and start that everlasting yarn with your chum the lunatic?

Bessie. I am not in a hurry to get home, father.

Carvil. Well, then, go steady with a poor blind man. Blind! Helpless! (Strikes the ground with his stick.) Never mind! I've had time to make enough money to have ham and eggs for breakfast every morning—thank God! And thank God, too, for it, girl. You haven't known a single hardship in all the days of your idle life. Unless you think that a blind, helpless father————-

Bessie. What is there for me to be in a hurry for?

Carvil. What did you say?

Bessie. I said there was nothing for me to hurry home for.

Carvil. There is, tho'. To yarn with a lunatic. Anything to get away from your duty.

Bessie. Captain Hagberd's talk never hurt you or anybody else.

Carvil. Go on. Stick up for your only friend.

Bessie. Is it my fault that I haven't another soul to speak to?

Carvil (Snarls). It's mine, perhaps. Can I help being blind? You fret because you want to be gadding about—with a helpless man left all alone at home. Your own father too.

Bessie. I haven't been away from you half a day since mother died.

Carvil (Viciously). He's a lunatic, our landlord is. That's what he is. Has been for years—long before those damned doctors destroyed my sight for me. (Growls angrily, then sighs.)

Bessie. Perhaps Captain Hagberd is not so mad as the town takes him for.

Carvil. (Grimly). Don't everybody know how he came here from the North to wait till his missing son turns up—here—of all places in the world. His boy that ran away to sea sixteen years ago and never did give a sign of life since! Don't I remember seeing people dodge round corners out of his way when he came along High Street. Seeing him, I tell you. (Groan.) He bothered everybody so with his silly talk of his son being sure to come back home—next year—next spring—next month————. What is it by this time, hey?

Bessie. Why talk about it? He bothers no one now.

Carvil. No. They've grown too fly. You've got only to pass a remark on his sail-cloth coat to make him shut up. All the town knows it. But he's got you to listen to his crazy talk whenever he chooses. Don't I hear you two at it, jabber, jabber, mumble, mumble————

Bessie. What is there so mad in keeping up hope?

Carvil (Scathing scorn). Not mad! Starving himself to lay money by—for that son. Filling his house with furniture he won't let anyone see—for that son. Advertising in the papers every week, these sixteen years—for that son. Not mad! Boy, he calls him. Boy Harry. His boy Harry. His lost boy Harry. Yah! Let him lose his sight to know what real trouble means. And the boy—the man, I should say—must 've been put away safe in Davy Jones's locker for many a year—drowned— food for fishes—dead.... Stands to reason, or he would have been here before, smelling around the old fool's money. (Shakes Bessie's arm slightly.) Hey?

Bessie. I don't know. May be.

Carvil (Bursting out). Damme if I don't think he ever had a son.

Bessie. Poor man. Perhaps he never had.

Carvil. Ain't that mad enough for you? But I suppose you think it sensible.

Bessie. What does it matter? His talk keeps him up.

Carvil. Aye! And it pleases you. Anything to get away from your poor blind father.... Jabber, jabber—mumble, mumble—till I begin to think you must be as crazy as he is. What do you find to talk about, you two? What's your game?

(During the scene Carvil and Bessie have crossed stage from L. to R. slowly with stoppages.)

Bessie. It's warm. Will you sit out for a while?

Carvil (Viciously). Yes, I will sit out. (Insistent.) But what can be your game? What are you up to? (They pass through garden gate.) Because if it's his money you are after————-

Bessie. Father! How can you!

Carvil (Disregarding her). To make you independent of your poor blind father, then you are a fool. (Drops heavily on seat.) He's too much of a miser to ever make a will—even if he weren't mad.

Bessie. Oh! It never entered my head. I swear it never did.

Carvil. Never did. Hey! Then you are a still bigger fool.... I want to go to sleep! (Takes off' his hat, drops it on ground, and leans his head back against the wall.)

Bessie. And I have been a good daughter to you. Won't you say that for me?

Carvil (Very distinctly). I want—to—go—to—sleep. I'm tired. (Closes his eyes.)

(During that scene Captain Hagberd has been seen hesitating at the back of stage, then running quickly to the door of his cottage. He puts inside a tin kettle (from under his coat) and comes down to the railing between the two gardens stealthily).

SCENE - II

Carvil seated. Bessie. Captain Hagberd (white beard, sail-cloth jacket).

Bessie (Knitting). You've been out this afternoon for quite a long time, haven't you?

Capt. Hagberd (Eager). Yes, my dear. (Slily) Of course you saw me come back.

Bessie. Oh, yes. I did see you. You had something under your coat.

Capt. H. (Anxiously). It was only a kettle, my dear. A tin water-kettle. I am glad I thought of it just in time. (Winks, nods.) When a husband gets back from his work he needs a lot of water for a wash. See? (Dignified.) Not that Harry'll ever need to do a hand's turn after he comes home... (Falters—casts stealthy glances on all sides).... tomorrow.

Bessie (Looks up, grave). Captain Hagberd, have you ever thought that perhaps your son will not. . .

Capt. H. (Paternally). I've thought of everything, my dear—of everything a reasonable young couple may need for housekeeping. Why, I can hardly turn about in my room up there, the house is that full. (Rubs his hands with satisfaction.) For my son Harry—when he comes home. One day more.

Bessie (Flattering). Oh, you are a great one for bargains. (Captain Hagberd delighted.) But, Captain Hagberd—if—if—you don't know what may happen—if all that home you've got together were to be wasted—for nothing—after all. (Aside.) Oh, I can't bring it out.

Capt. H. (Agitated; flings arms up, stamps feet; stuttering). What? What d'ye mean? What's going to happen to the things?

Bessie (Soothing). Nothing! Nothing! Dust—or moth—you know. Damp, perhaps. You never let anyone into the house . . .

Capt. H. Dust! Damp! (Has a throaty, gurgling laugh.) I light the fires and dust the things myself. (Indignant.) Let anyone into the house, indeed! What would Harry say! (Walks up and down his garden hastily with tosses, jings, and jerks of his whole body.)

Bessie (With authority.) Now, then, Captain Hagberd! You know I won't put up with your tantrums. (Shakes finger at him.)

Capt. H. (Subdued, but still sulky, with his back to her). You want to see the things. That's what you're after. Well, no, not even you. Not till Harry has had his first look.

Bessie. Oh, no! I don't. (Relenting.) Not till you're willing. (Smiles at Capt. H., who has turned half round already!) You mustn't excite yourself. (Knits.)

Capt. H. (Condescending). And you the only sensible girl for miles and miles around. Can't you trust me? I am a domestic man. Always was, my dear. I hated the sea. People don't know what they let their boys into when they send them to sea. As soon make convicts of them at once. What sort of life is it? Most of your time you don't know what's going on at home. (Insinuating.) There's nothing anywhere on earth as good as a home, my dear. (Pause.) With a good husband...

Carvil (Heard from his seat fragmentarily). There they go... jabber, jabber... mumble, mumble. (With a groaning effort?) Helpless!

Capt. H. (Mutters). Extravagant ham and eggs fellow. (Louder.) Of course it isn't as if he had a son to make a home ready for. Girls are different, my dear. They don't run away, my dear, my dear. (Agitated.)

Bessie (Drops her arms wearily). No, Captain Hagberd—they don't.

Capt. H. (Slowly). I wouldn't let my own flesh and blood go to sea. Not I.

Bessie. And the boy ran away.

Capt. H. (A little vacantly). Yes, my only son Harry. (Rouses himself.) Coming home to-morrow.

Bessie (Speaks softly). Sometimes, Captain Hagberd, a hope turns out false.

Capt. H. (Uneasy). What's that got to do with Harry's coming back?

Bessie. It's good to hope for something. But suppose now———-
(Feeling her way.) Yours is not the only lost son that's never...

Capt. H. Never what! You don't believe he's drowned. (Crouches,
glaring and grasping the rails.)

Bessie (Frightened, drops knitting). Captain Hagberd—don't.
(Catches hold of his shoulders over the railings?) Don't—my God! He's
going out of his mind! (Cries.) I didn't mean it! I don't know.

Capt. H. (Has backed away. An affected burst of laughter). What
nonsense. None of us Hagberds belonged to the sea. All farmers for
hundreds of years, (fraternal and cunning?) Don't alarm yourself, my
dear. The sea can't get us. Look at me! I didn't get drowned. Moreover,
Harry ain't a sailor at all. And if he isn't a sailor, he's bound to come
back—to-morrow.

Bessie (Has been facing him; murmurs). No. I give it up. He scares me.
(Aloud, sharply.) Then I would give up that advertising in the papers.

Capt. H. (Surprised and puzzled). Why, my dear? Everybody does it.
His poor mother and I have been advertising for years and years. But
she was an impatient woman. She died.

Bessie. If your son's coming, as—as you say—what's the good of that
expense? You had better spend that half-crown on yourself. I believe
you don't eat enough.

Capt. H. (Confused). But it's the right thing to do. Look at the Sunday
papers. Missing relatives on top page—all proper. (Looks unhappy.)

Bessie (Tartly). Ah, well! I declare I don't know what you live on.

Capt. H. Are you getting impatient, my dear? Don't get impatient—
like my poor wife. If she'd only been patient she'd be here. Waiting. Only
one day more. (Pleadingly.) Don't be impatient, my dear.

Bessie. I've no patience with you sometimes.

Capt. H. (Flash of lucidity). Why? What's the matter? (Sympathetic.)
You're tired out, my dear, that's what it is.

Bessie. Yes, I am. Day after day. (Stands listless, arms hanging down.)

Capt. H. (Timidly). House dull?

Bessie (Apathetic). Yes.

Capt. H. (As before). H'm. Wash, cook, scrub. Hey?

Bessie (As before). Yes.

Capt. H. (Pointing stealthily at the sleeping Carvil). Heavy?

Bessie. (In a dead voice). Like a millstone.

(A silence.)

Capt. H. (Burst of indignation). Why don't that extravagant fellow get you a servant?

Bessie. I don't know.

Capt. H. (Cheerily). Wait till Harry comes home. He'll get you one.

Bessie (Almost hysterical; laughs). Why, Captain Hagberd, perhaps your son won't even want to look at me—when he comes home.

Capt. H. (In a great voice). What! (Quite low.) The boy wouldn't dare. (Rising choler.) Wouldn't dare to refuse the only sensible girl for miles around. That stubborn jackanapes refuse to marry a girl like you! (Walks about in a fury.) You trust me, my dear, my dear, my dear. I'll make him. I'll—I'll ————— (Splutters.) Cut him off with a shilling.

Bessie. Hush! (Severe.) You mustn't talk like that. What's this? More of your tantrums?

Capt. H. (Quite humble). No, no—this isn't my tantrums—when I don't feel quite well in my head. Only I can't stand this... I've grown as fond of you as if you'd been the wife of my Harry already.

And to be told————— (Cant restrain himself; shouts.)

Jackanapes!

Bessie. Sh————! Don't you worry! (Wearily.)

I must give that up too, I suppose. (Aloud.) I didn't mean it, Captain Hagberd.

Capt. H. It's as if I were to have two children to-morrow. My son Harry—and the only sensible girl—————. Why, my dear, I couldn't get on without you. We two are reasonable together. The rest of the people in this town are crazy. The way they stare at you. And the grins—they're all on the grin. It makes me dislike to go out. (Bewildered.) It seems as if there was something wrong about—somewhere. My dear, is there anything wrong—you who are sensible.. .

Bessie (Soothingly tender). No, no, Captain Hagberd. There is nothing wrong about you anywhere.

Carvil (Lying back). Bessie! (Sits up.) Get my hat, Bessie.... Bessie, my hat.... Bessie.... Bessie. ...

(At the first sound Bessie picks up and puts away her knitting. She walks towards him, picks up hat, puts it on his head).

Bessie, my... (Hat on head; shouting stops.) Bessie. (Quietly). Will you go in, now? Carvil. Help me up. Steady. I'm dizzy. It's the thundery weather. An autumn thunderstorm means a bad gale. Very fierce—and sudden. There will be shipwrecks to-night on our coast.

(Exit Bessie and Carvil through door of their cottage. It has fallen dusk.)

Capt. H. (Picks up spade). Extravagant fellow! And all this town is mad—perfectly mad. I found them out years ago. Thank God they don't come this way staring and grinning. I can't bear them. I'll never go again into that High Street. (Agitated.) Never, never, never. Won't need to after to-morrow. Never! (Flings down spade in passion.)

(While Hagberd speaks, the bow window of the Carvils is lit up, and Bessie is seen settling her father in a big armchair. Pulls down blind. Enter Lamplighter. Capt. H. picks up the spade and leans forward on it with both hands; very still, watching him light the lamp.)

Lamplighter (Jocular). There! You will be able to dig by lamplight if the fancy takes you.

(Exit Lamplighter to back.)

Capt. H. (Disgusted). Ough! The people here. . . (Shudders.)

Lamplighter's Voice (Heard loudly beyond the cottages). Yes, that's the way.

(Enter Harry from back.)

SCENE - III

(Capt. H. Harry. Later Bessie)

Harry Hagberd (thirty-one, tall, broad shoulders, shaven face, small moustache. Blue serge suit. Coat open. Grey flannel shirt without collar and tie. No waistcoat. Belt with buckle. Black, soft felt hat, wide-brimmed, worn crushed in the crown and a little on one side. Good nature, recklessness, some swagger in the bearing. Assured, deliberate walk with a heavy tread. Slight roll in the gait. Walks down. Stops, hands in pockets. Looks about. Speaks.) This must be it. Can't see anything beyond. There's somebody. (Walks up to Capt. Hagberd's gate?) Can you tell me... (Manner changes. Leans elbow on gate?) Why, you must be Capt. Hagberd himself.

Capt. H. (In garden, both hands on spade, peering, startled). Yes, I am.

Harry (Slowly). You've been advertising in the papers for your son, I believe.

Capt. H. (Off his guard, nervous). Yes. My only boy Harry. He's coming home to-morrow. (Mumbles.) For a permanent stay.

Harry (Surprised). The devil he is! (Change of tone?) My word! You've grown a beard like Father Christmas himself.

Capt. H. (Impressively). Go your way. (Waves one hand loftily?) What's that to you. Go your way. (Agitated?) Go your way.

Harry. There, there. I am not trespassing in the street—where I stand—am I? Tell you what, I fancy there's something wrong about your news. Suppose you let me come in—for a quiet chat, you know.

Capt. H. (Horrified). Let you—you come in!

Harry (Persuasive). Because I could give you some real information about your son. The—very—latest—tip. If you care to hear.

One Day More A Play In One Act

Capt. H. (Explodes). No! I don't care to hear. (Begins to pace to and fro, spade on shoulder. Gesticulating with his other arm.) Here's a fellow—a grinning town fellow, who says there's something wrong. (Fiercely.) I have got more information than you're aware of. I have all the information I want. I have had it for years—for years—for years—enough to last me till to-morrow! Let you come in, indeed! What would Harry say?

(Bessie Carvil appears at cottage door with a white wrap on her head and stands in her garden trying to see).

Bessie. What's the matter?

Capt. H. (Beside himself). An information fellow. (Stumbles.)

Harry (Putting out arm to steady him, gravely). Here! Steady a bit! Seems to me somebody's been trying to get at you. (Change of tone.) Hullo! What's this rig you've got on?... Storm canvas coat, by George! (He gives a frig, throaty laugh.) Well! You are a character!

Capt. H. (Daunted by the allusion, looks at coat). I—I wear it for—for the time being. Till—till—to-morrow. (Shrinks away, spade in hand, to door of his cottage.)

Bessie (Advancing). And what may you want, sir?

Harry (Turns to Bessie at once; easy manner). I'd like to know about this swindle that's going to be sprung on him. I didn't mean to startle the old man. You see, on my way here I dropped into a barber's to get a twopenny shave, and they told me there that he was something of a character. He has been a character all his life.

Bessie (Wondering). What swindle?

Capt. H. A grinning fellow! (Makes sudden dash indoors with the spade. Door slams. Affected gurgling laugh within.)

SCENE - IV

(Bessie and Harry. Later Capt. H. from window)

Harry (After a short silence). What on earth's upset him so? What's the meaning of all this fuss? He isn't always like that, is he?

Bessie. I don't know who you are; but I may tell you that his mind has been troubled for years about an only son who ran away from home—a long time ago. Everybody knows that here.

Harry (Thoughtful). Troubled—for years! (Suddenly.) Well, I am the son.

Bessie (Steps back). You! . .. Harry!

Harry (Amused, dry tone). Got hold of my name, eh? Been making friends with the old man?

Bessie (Distressed). Yes... I... sometimes. . . (Rapidly!) He's our landlord.

Harry (Scornfully). Owns both them rabbit hutches, does he? Just a thing he'd be proud of... (Earnest.) And now you had better tell me all about that chap who's coming to-morrow. Know anything of him? I reckon there's more than one in that little game. Come! Out with it! (Chaffing.) I don't take no... from women.

Bessie (Bewildered). Oh! It's so difficult... What had I better do?...

Harry (Good-humoured). Make a clean breast of it.

Bessie (Wildly to herself). Impossible! (Starts.) You don't understand. I must think—see—try to—I, I must have time. Plenty of time.

Harry. What for? Come. Two words. And don't be afraid for yourself. I ain't going to make it a police job. But it's the other fellow that'll get upset when he least expects it. There'll be some fun when he shows his mug here to-morrow. (Snaps fingers.) I don't care that for the old man's dollars, but right is right. You shall see me put a head on that coon, whoever he is.

Bessie (Wrings hands slightly). What had I better do? (Suddenly to Harry.) It's you—you yourself that we—that he's waiting for. It's you who are to come to-morrow.

Harry (Slowly). Oh! it's me! (Perplexed.) There's something there I can't understand. I haven't written ahead or anything. It was my chum who showed me the advertisement with the old boy's address, this very morning—in London.

Bessie (Anxious). How can I make it plain to you without... (Bites her lip, embarrassed.) Sometimes he talks so strangely.

Harry (Expectant). Does he? What about?

Bessie. Only you. And he will stand no contradicting.

Harry. Stubborn. Eh? The old man hasn't changed much from what I can remember. (They stand looking at each other helplessly.)

Bessie. He's made up his mind you would come back . . . to-morrow.

Harry. I can't hang about here till morning. Got no money to get a bed. Not a cent. But why won't to-day do?

Bessie. Because you've been too long away.

Harry (With force). Look here, they fairly drove me out. Poor mother nagged at me for being idle, and the old man said he would cut my soul out of my body rather than let me go to sea.

Bessie (Murmurs). He can bear no contradicting.

Harry (Continuing). Well, it looked as tho' he would do it too. So I went. (Moody.) It seems to me sometimes I was born to them by a mistake... in that other rabbit hutch of a house.

Bessie (A little mocking). And where do you think you ought to have been born by rights?

Harry. In the open—upon a beach—on a windy night.

Bessie (Faintly). Ah!

Harry. They were characters, both of them, by George! Shall I try the door?

Bessie. Wait. I must explain to you why it is to-morrow.

Harry. Aye. That you must, or...

(Window in H.'s cottage runs up.)

Capt. H.'s Voice (Above). A—grinning—information—fellow coming to worry me in my own garden! What next?

(Window rumbles down.)

Bessie. Yes. I must. (Lays hand on Harry's sleeve.) Let's get further off. Nobody ever comes this way after dark.

Harry (Careless laugh). Aye. A good road for a walk with a girl.

(They turn their backs on audience and move up the stage slowly. Close together. Harry bends his head over Bessie).

Bessie's Voice (Beginning eagerly). People here somehow did not take kindly to him.

Harry's Voice. Aye. Aye. I understand that.

(They walk slowly back towards the front.)

Bessie. He was almost ready to starve himself for your sake.

Harry. And I had to starve more than once for his whim.

Bessie. I'm afraid you've a hard heart. (Remains thoughtful.)

Harry. What for? For running away? (Indignant.) Why, he wanted to make a blamed lawyer's clerk of me.

(From here this scene goes on mainly near and about the street lamp.)

Bessie (Rousing herself). What are you? A sailor?

Harry. Anything you like. (Proudly.) Sailor enough to be worth my salt on board any craft that swims the seas.

Bessie. He will never, never believe it. He mustn't be contradicted.

Harry. Always liked to have his own way. And you've been encouraging him.

Bessie (Earnestly). No!—not in everything—not really!

Harry (Vexed laugh). What about that pretty tomorrow notion? I've a hungry chum in London—waiting for me.

Bessie (Defending herself). Why should I make the poor old friendless man miserable? I thought you were far away. I thought you were dead. I didn't know but you had never been born. I... I... (Harry turns to her. She desperately.) It was easier to believe it myself. (Carried away.) And after all it's true. It's come to pass. This is the to-morrow we've been waiting for.

Harry (Half perfunctorily). Aye. Anybody can see that your heart is as soft as your voice.

Bessie (As if unable to keep back the words). I didn't think you would have noticed my voice.

Harry (Already inattentive). H'm. Dashed scrape. This is a queer to-morrow, without any sort of today, as far as I can see. (Resolutely.) I must try the door.

Bessie. Well—try, then.

Harry (From gate looking over shoulder at Bessie). He ain't likely to fly out at me, is he? I would be afraid of laying my hands on him. The chaps are always telling me I don't know my own strength.

Bessie (In front). He's the most harmless creature that ever. ..

Harry. You wouldn't say so if you had seen him walloping me with a hard leather strap. (Walking up garden.) I haven't forgotten it in sixteen long years. (Rat-tat-tat twice.) Hullo, Dad. (Bessie intensely expectant. Rat-tat-tat.) Hullo, Dad—let me in. I am your own Harry. Straight. Your son Harry come back home—a day too soon.

(Window above rumbles up.)

Capt. H. (Seen leaning out, aiming with spade). Aha! Bessie (Warningly). Look out, Harry! (Spade falls.) Are you hurt? (Window rumbles down.) Harry (In the distance). Only grazed my hat.

Bessie. Thank God! (Intensely.) What'll he do now?

Harry (Comes forward, slamming gate behind him). Just like old times. Nearly licked the life out of me for wanting to go away, and now I come back he shies a confounded old shovel at my head. (Fumes. Laughs a little). I wouldn't care, only poor little Ginger—Ginger's my chum up in London—he will starve while I walk back all the way from here. (Faces Bessie blankly.) I spent my last twopence on a shave. ... Out of respect for the old man.

Bessie. I think, if you let me, I could manage to talk him round in a week, maybe.

(A muffled periodical bellowing had been heard faintly for some time.)

Harry (On the alert). What's this? Who's making this row? Hark! Bessie, Bessie. It's in your house, I believe.

Bessie (Without stirring, drearily). It's for me.

Harry (Discreetly, whispering). Good voice for a ship's deck in a squall. Your husband? (Steps out of lamplight.)

Bessie. No. My father. He's blind. (Pause). I'm not married.

(Bellowings grow louder.)

Harry. Oh, I say. What's up? Who's murdering him?

Bessie (Calmly). I expect he's finished his tea. (Bellowing continues regularly.)

Harry. Hadn't you better see to it? You'll have the whole town coming out here presently. (Bessie moves off.) I say! (Bessie stops.) Couldn't you scare up some bread and butter for me from that tea? I'm hungry. Had no breakfast.

Bessie (Starts off at the word "hungry," dropping to the ground the white woollen shawl). I won't be a minute. Don't go away.

Harry (Alone; picks up shawl absently, and, looking at it spread out in his hands, pronounces slowly). A—dam'—silly—scrape. (Pause. Throws shawl on arm. Strolls up and down. Mutters.) No money to get back. (Louder.) Silly little Ginger'll think I've got hold of the pieces and given an old shipmate the go by. One good shove—(Makes motion of bursting in door with his shoulders)—would burst that door in—I bet. (Looks about.) I wonder where the nearest bobby is! No. They would want to bundle me neck and crop into chokey. (Shudders.) Perhaps. It makes me dog sick to think of being locked up. Haven't got the nerve. Not for prison. (Leans against lamp-post.) And not a cent for my fare. I wonder if that girl now...

Bessie (Coming hastily forward, plate with bread and meat in hand). I didn't take time to get anything else....

Harry (Begins to eat). You're not standing treat to a beggar. My dad is a rich man—you know.

Bessie (Plate in hand). You resemble your father.

Harry. I was the very image of him in face from a boy—(Eats)—and that's about as far as it goes. He was always one of your domestic characters. He looked sick when he had to go to sea for a fortnight's trip. (Laughs.) He was all for house and home.

Bessie. And you? Have you never wished for a home? (Goes off with empty plate and puts it down hastily on Carvil's bench—out of sight.)

Harry (Left in front). Home! If I found myself shut up in what the old man calls a home, I would kick it down about my ears on the third day—or else go to bed and die before the week was out. Die in a house—ough!

Bessie (Returning; stops and speaks from garden railing). And where is it that you would wish to die?

Harry. In the bush, in the sea, on some blamed mountain-top for choice. No such luck, tho', I suppose.

Bessie (From distance). Would that be luck? Harry. Yes! For them that make the whole world their home.

Bessie (Comes forward shyly). The world's a cold home—they say.

Harry (A little gloomy). So it is. When a man's done for.

Bessie. You see! (Taunting). And a ship's not so very big after all.

Harry. No. But the sea is great. And then what of the ship! You love her and leave her, Miss—Bessie's your name—isn't it?... I like that name.

Bessie. You like my name! I wonder you remembered it.... That's why, I suppose.

Harry (Slight swagger in voice). What's the odds! As long as a fellow has lived. And a voyage isn't a marriage—as we sailors say.

Bessie. So you're not married—(Movement of Harry)—to any ship.

Harry (Soft laugh). Ship! I've loved and left more of them than I can remember. I've been nearly everything you can think of but a tinker or a soldier; I've been a boundary rider; I've sheared sheep and humped my swag and harpooned a whale; I've rigged ships and skinned dead bullocks and prospected for gold—and turned my back on more money than the old man would have scraped together in his whole life.

Bessie (Thoughtfully). I could talk him over in a week.. . .

Harry (Negligently). I dare say you could. (Joking.) I don't know but what I could make shift to wait if you only promise to talk to me now and then. I've grown quite fond of your voice. I like a right woman's voice.

Bessie (Averted head). Quite fond! (Sharply.) Talk! Nonsense! Much you'd care. (Businesslike.) Of course I would have to sometimes.... (Thoughtful again.) Yes. In a week—if—if only I knew you would try to get on with him afterwards.

Harry (Leaning against lamp-post; growls through his teeth). More humouring. Ah! well, no! (Hums significantly)

Oh, oh, oh, Rio, . . .

And fare thee well

My bonnie young girl,

We're bound for Rio Grande.

Bessie (Shivering). What's this?

Harry. Why! The chorus of an up-anchor tune. Kiss and go. A deep-water ship's good-bye.... You are cold. Here's that thing of yours I've picked up and forgot there on my arm. Turn round a bit. So. (Wraps her up—commanding.) Hold the ends together in front.

Bessie (Softly). A week is not so very long.

Harry (Begins violently). You think that I————-

(Stops with sidelong look at her.) I can't dodge about in ditches and live on air and water. Can I? I haven't any money—you know.

Bessie. He's been scraping and saving up for years. All he has is for you, and perhaps...

Harry (Interrupts). Yes. If I come to sit on it like a blamed toad in a hole. Thank you.

Bessie (Angrily). What did you come for, then?

Harry (Promptly). For five quid—(Pause.)—after a jolly good spree.

Bessie (Scathingly). You and that—that—chum of yours have been drinking.

Harry (Laughs). Don't fly out, Miss Bessie—dear. Ginger's not a bad little chap. Can't take care of himself, tho'. Blind three days. (Serious.) Don't think I am given that way. Nothing and nobody can get over me unless I like. I can be as steady as a rock.

Bessie (Murmurs). Oh! I don't think you are bad.

Harry (Approvingly). You're right there. (Impulsive.) Ask the girls all over————-(Checks himself.) Ginger, he's long-headed, too, in his way—mind you. He sees the paper this morning, and says he to me, 'Hallo! Look at that, Harry—loving parent—that's five quid, sure.' So we scraped all our pockets for the fare....

Bessie (Unbelieving). You came here for that.

Harry (Surprised). What else would I want here? Five quid isn't much to ask for—once in sixteen years. (Through his teeth with a sidelong look at B.) And now I am ready to go—for my fare.

Bessie (Clasping her hands). Whoever heard a man talk like this before! I can't believe you mean it?

Harry. What? That I would go? You just try and see.

Bessie (Disregarding him). Don't you care for anyone? Didn't you ever want anyone in the world to care for you?

Harry. In the world! (Boastful.) There's hardly a place you can go in the world where you wouldn't find somebody that did care for Harry Hagberd. (Pause.) I'm not of the sort that go about skulking under false names.

Bessie. Somebody—that means a woman.

Harry. Well! And if it did.

Bessie (Unsteadily). Oh, I see how it is. You get round them with your soft speeches, your promises, and then...

Harry (Violently). Never!

Bessie (Startled, steps back). Ah—you never. . .

Harry (Calm). Never yet told a lie to a woman.

Bessie. What lie?

Harry. Why, the lie that comes glib to a man's tongue. None of that for me. I leave the sneaking off to them soft-spoken chaps you're thinking of. No! If you love me you take me. And if you take me—why, then, the capstan-song of deep-water ships is sure to settle it all some fine day.

Bessie (After a short pause, with effort). It's like your ships, then.

Harry (Amused). Exactly, up to now. Or else I wouldn't be here in a silly fix.

Bessie (Assumed indifference). Perhaps it's because you've never yet met———- (Voice fails.)

Harry (Negligently). Maybe. And perhaps never shall.... What's the odds? It's the looking for a thing.... No matter. I love them all—ships and women. The scrapes they got me into, and the scrapes they got me out of—my word! I say, Miss Bessie, what are you thinking of?

Bessie (Lifts her head). That you are supposed never to tell a lie.

Harry. Never, eh? You wouldn't be that hard on a chap.

Bessie (Recklessly). Never to a woman, I mean.

Harry. Well, no. (Serious.) Never anything that matters. (Aside.) I don't seem to get any nearer to my railway fare. (Leans wearily against the lamppost with a far-off look. B. looks at him.)

Bessie. Now what are you thinking of?

Harry (Turns his head; stares at B.). Well, I was thinking what a fine figure of a girl you are.

Bessie (Looks away a moment). Is that true, or is it only one of them that don't matter?

Harry (Laughing a little). No! no! That's true. Haven't you ever been told that before? The men...

Bessie. I hardly speak to a soul from year's end to year's end. Father's blind. He don't like strangers, and he can't bear to think of me out of his call. Nobody comes near us much.

Harry (Absent-minded). Blind—ah! of course.

Bessie. For years and years . . .

Harry (Commiserating). For years and years. In one of them hutches. You are a good daughter. (Brightening up.) A fine girl altogether. You seem the sort that makes a good chum to a man in a fix. And there's not a man in this whole town who found you out? I can hardly credit it, Miss Bessie. (B. shakes her head.) Man I said! (Contemptuous.) A lot of tame rabbits in hutches I call them.... (Breaks off.) I say, when's the last train up to London? Can you tell me?

Bessie (Gazes at him steadily). What for? You've no money.

Harry. That's just it. (Leans back against post again.) Hard luck. (Insinuating.) But there was never a time in all my travels that a woman of the right sort did not turn up to help me out of a fix. I don't know why. It's perhaps because they know without telling that I love them all. (Playful.) I've almost fallen in love with you, Miss Bessie.

Bessie (Unsteady laugh). Why! How you talk! You haven't even seen my face properly. (One step towards H., as if compelled.)

Harry (Bending forward gallantly). A little pale. It suits some. (Puts out his hand, catches hold of B.'s arm. Draws her to him.) Let's see.... Yes, it suits you. (It's a moment before B. puts up her hands, palms out, and turns away her head.)

Bessie (Whispering). Don't. (Struggles a little. Released, stands averted.)

Harry. No offence. (Stands, back to audience, looking at H.'s cottage.)

Bessie (Alone in front; faces audience; whispers). My voice—my figure—my heart—my face....

(A silence. B.'s face gradually lights up. Directly H. speaks, expression of hopeful attention.)

Harry (From railings). The old man seems to have gone to sleep waiting for that to-morrow of his.

Bessie. Come away. He sleeps very little.

Harry (Strolls down). He has taken an everlasting jamming hitch round the whole business. (Vexed.) Cast it loose who may. (Contemptuous exclamation.) To-morrow. Pooh! It'll be just another mad today.

Bessie. It's the brooding over his hope that's done it. People teased him so. It's his fondness for you that's troubled his mind.

Harry. Aye. A confounded shovel on the head. The old man had always a queer way of showing his fondness for me.

Bessie. A hopeful, troubled, expecting old man—left alone—all alone.

Harry (Lower tone). Did he ever tell you what mother died of?

Bessie. Yes. (A little bitter.) From impatience.

Harry (Makes a gesture with his arm; speaks vaguely but with feeling). I believe you have been very good to my old man....

Bessie (Tentative). Wouldn't you try to be a son to him?

Harry (Angrily). No contradicting; is that it? You seem to know my dad pretty well. And so do I. He's dead nuts on having his own way— and I've been used to have my own too long. It's the deuce of a fix.

Bessie. How could it hurt you not to contradict him for a while—and perhaps in time you would get used. ..

Harry (Interrupts sulkily). I ain't accustomed to knuckle under. There's a pair of us. Hagberd's both. I ought to be thinking of my train.

Bessie (Earnestly). Why? There's no need. Let us get away up the road a little.

Harry (Through his teeth). And no money for the fare. (Looks up.) Sky's come overcast. Black, too. It'll be a wild, windy night... to walk the high road on. But I and wild nights are old friends wherever the free wind blows.

Bessie (Entreating). No need. No need. (Looks apprehensively at Hagberd's cottage. Takes a couple of steps up as if to draw Harry further off. Harry follows. Both stop.)

Harry (After waiting). What about this tomorrow whim?

Bessie. Leave that to me. Of course all his fancies are not mad. They aren't. (Pause.) Most people in this town would think what he had set his mind on quite sensible. If he ever talks to you of it, don't contradict him. It would—it would be dangerous.

Harry (Surprised). What would he do?

Bessie. He would—I don't know—something rash.

Harry (Startled). To himself?

Bessie. No. It'd be against you—I fear.

Harry (Sullen). Let him.

Bessie. Never. Don't quarrel. But perhaps he won't even try to talk to you of it. (Thinking aloud.) Who knows what I can do with him in a week! I can, I can, I can—I must.

Harry. Come—what's this sensible notion of his that I mustn't quarrel about?

Bessie (Turns to Harry, calm, forcible). If I make him once see that you've come back, he will be as sane as you or I. All his mad notions will be gone. But that other is quite sensible. And you mustn't quarrel over it.

(Moves up to back of stage. Harry follows a little behind, away from audience.)

Harry's Voice (Calm). Let's hear what it is.

(Voices cease. Action visible as before. Harry steps back and walks hastily down. Bessie at his elbow, follows with her hands clasped?)

(Loud burst of voice.)

Harry (Raving to and fro). No! Expects me—a home. Who wants his home?... What I want is hard work, or an all-fired racket, or more room than there is in the whole of England. Expects me! A man like me—for his rotten money—there ain't enough money in the world to turn me into a blamed tame rabbit in a hutch. (He stops suddenly before Bessie, arms crossed on breast. Violently.) Don't you see it?

Bessie (Terrified, stammering faintly). Yes. Yes. Don't look at me like this. (Sudden scream.) Don't quarrel with him. He's mad!

Harry (Headlong utterance). Mad! Not he. He likes his own way. Tie me up by the neck here. Here! Ha! Ha! Ha! (Louder.) And the whole world is not a bit too big for me to spread my elbows in, I can tell you—what's your name—Bessie. (Rising scorn). Marry! Wants me to marry and settle.... (Scathingly.) And as likely as not he has looked out the girl too—dash my soul. Talked to you about it—did he? And do you happen to know the Judy—may I ask?

(Window in Hagberd's cottage runs up. They start and stand still.)

Capt. H. (Above, begins slowly). A grinning information fellow from a crazy town. (Voice changes.) Bessie, I see you. . . .

Bessie (Shrill). Captain Hagberd! Say nothing. You don't understand. For heaven's sake don't.

Capt. H. Send him away this minute, or I will tell Harry. They know nothing of Harry in this crazy town. Harry's coming home to-morrow. Do you hear? One day more!

(Silence.)

Harry (Mutters). Well!—he is a character.

Capt. H. (Chuckles softly). Never you fear! The boy shall marry you. (Sudden anger.) He'll have to. I'll make him. Or, if not—(Furious)—I'll cut him off with a shilling, and leave everything to you. Jackanapes! Let him starve!

(Window rumbles down.)

Harry (Slowly). So it's you—the girl. It's you! Now I begin to see.... By heavens, you have a heart as soft as your woman's voice.

Bessie (Half averted, face in hands). You see! Don't come near me.

Harry (Makes a step towards her). I must have another look at your pale face.

Bessie (Turns unexpectedly and pushes him with both hands; Harry staggers back and stands still; Bessie, fiercely). Go away.

Harry (Watching her). Directly. But women always had to get me out of my scrapes. I am a beggar now, and you must help me out of my scrape.

Bessie (Who at the word "beggar" had begun fumbling in the pocket of her dress, speaks wildly). Here it is. Take it. Don't look at me. Don't speak to me!

Harry (Swaggers up under the lamp; looks at coin in his palm). Half-a-quid. . .. My fare!

Bessie (Hands clenched). Why are you still here?

Harry. Well, you are a fine figure of a girl. My word. I've a good mind to stop—for a week.

Bessie (Pain and shame). Oh!.... What are you waiting for? If I had more money I would give it all, all. I would give everything I have to make you go—to make you forget you had ever heard my voice and seen my face. (Covers face with hands.)

Harry (Sombre, watches her). No fear! I haven't forgotten a single one of you in the world. Some've given me more than money. No matter. You can't buy me in—and you can't buy yourself out. . .

(Strides towards her. Seizes her arms. Short struggle. Bessie gives way. Hair falls loose. H. kisses her forehead, cheeks, lips, then releases her. Bessie staggers against railings.)

(Exit Harry; measured walk without haste)

Bessie (Staring eyes, hair loose, back against railings; calls out). Harry! (Gathers up her skirts and runs a little way) Come back, Harry. (Staggers forward against lamp-post) Harry! (Much lower) Harry! (In a whisper) Take me with you. (Begins to laugh, at first faintly, then louder.)

(Window rumbles up, and Capt. H.'s chuckle mingles with Bessie's laughter, which abruptly stops.)

Capt. H. (Goes on chuckling; speaks cautiously). Is he gone yet, that information fellow? Do you see him anywhere, my dear?

Bessie (Low and stammering). N-no, no! (Totters away from lamp-post) I don't see him.

Capt. H. (Anxious). A grinning vagabond, my dear. Good girl. It's you who drove him away. Good girl.

(Stage gradually darkens)

Bessie. Go in; be quiet! You have done harm enough.

Capt. H. (Alarmed). Why. Do you hear him yet, my dear?

Bessie (Sobs, drooping against the railings). No! No! I don't. I don't hear him any more.

Capt. H. (Triumphant). Now we shall be all right, my dear, till our Harry comes home to-morrow. (Affected gurgling laugh.)

Bessie (Distracted). Be quiet. Shut yourself in. You will make me mad. (Losing control of herself, repeats with rising infection) You make me mad.

(With despair) There is no to-morrow! (Sinks to ground near middle railings. Low sobs)

(Stage darkens perceptibly.)

Capt. H. (Above, in a voice suddenly dismayed and shrill).

What! What do you say, my dear? No to-morrow? (Broken, very feebly.) No—to-morrow?

(Window runs down)

Carvil (Heard within, muffled bellowing). Bessie—Bessie—Bessie—Bessie———— (At the first call Bessie springs up and begins to stumble blindly towards the door. A faint fash of lightnings followed by a very low rumble of thunder) You!—Bessie!

CURTAIN

THE END